# 7 Keys to Keep Your Cup Filled

_LaTrice Williams_

*BE FILLED AND REMAIN FULL IN JESUS NAME!*

# AUTHOR'S CONTACT INFO

Email:
LaTriceSpeaks@latricewilliams.com

Main Website:
www.latricewilliams.com

Facebook:
www.facebook.com/TheDestinyDriver/

Twitter:
https://www.twitter.com/DestinyDriverLW

Instagram:
www.instagram.com/thedestinydriver/

# ACKNOWLEDGMENT

Thank you, dear Reader Friends who continue to support this avenue of ministry, through your purchases and sharing of my work! You are appreciated and loved!

Thank you, Beta Readers who help me, to continue to bring to life the work assigned to me for the Kingdom. Your work is greatly appreciated!

Thank you, Friends and Family, for your support and love!

Most important, Thank You Big God, my Father for continuing to download into Your people!

# *INTRODUCTION*

This book began with a glass of water!

I was on assignment in a prayer intensive workshop with one of my Spiritual Daughters. During that class, we were discussing fasting and prayer. While I was in the class, I was drinking water. I had a glass of water and a bottle. I drank both of them, so I got up to grab another bottle. I said I'll grab another bottle – real quick! Don't miss that. I like cold water but when I reached in the refrigerator, I realized I had drunk all of the cold bottled water. But I also have a decanter of water, so I grabbed it to pour another glass.

As I was pouring, I heard Holy Spirit say - Keep Your Cup Filled! I also heard Him say - you don't need something quick, just keep pouring the water! Meaning there is water that you have access to, and even though it's not as quick because you have to grab the glass and grab the water canister, you don't need what's quick. God said to me – you need to keep *pouring* the water and keep your cup filled. I realized that keeping my cup filled meant I wouldn't run out of water. When I needed or wanted it, it was on hand. It was available at the moment that I needed it. I didn't have to seek it out, it was there!

I began to pray and ask God what more was He saying about this cup. The Lord began to say that many of His people are living from an empty cup. Some are living from a half-filled cup. Because of that, they feel empty, void, unfulfilled, and unaccomplished. It's because they are living without the continual flow of God in their lives. They are missing this flow of God because they've failed to keep their cup

1

full!

This book is for people who know there's something more that you need, but can't seem to tap into it. It's for those people whose capacity has been diminished because there has been no stretching, no discipline, no intentionality, and no fellowship with God as it should be.

There is a song by CeCe Winans that I love called *Fill My Cup*. The song lyrics are – "fill my cup Lord, I lift it up Lord. Come and quench this thirsting in my soul. Bread from Heaven, feed me til' I want no more. Fill my cup Lord, fill it up and make me whole."

On the day God downloaded this book to me, I was humming this song and the Lord said very clearly to me – YOU FILL IT!

Here's the thing - relationship with God is not one sided. God will fill us if we'll lift our cup up to Him. But what does lifting our cup before God look like?

As a result of that glass of water I was seeking, God gave me seven keys to keep our cups filled! These seven keys will unlock things within us so that we are able to fill our cup. Seven things that He will respond to and release what we need so that our cup remains full, and when we need it, it's available!

There are some things that we want God to do, however, there are some things we need to do. A continuously filled cup requires some action on our part.

Let's get into it! Keep Your Cup Filled! This is how we keep pouring the water of the living God!

# KEY ONE
## *Prayer*

The first key to keep our cup filled is prayer!

*1 Thessalonians 5:17 NLT – Never Stop Praying.*

*Ephesians 6:18 TLB - Pray all the time. Ask God for anything in line with the Holy Spirit's wishes. Plead with Him, reminding Him of your needs, and keep praying earnestly for all Christians everywhere.*

Prayer is the number 1 key of keeping our cups filled. Those are the instructions, but what does that look like? To never stop praying and pray all the time is simply keeping the conversation between you and God open and flowing. It means talking to God and actively listening to Him. It means spending some time away, alone with Him. It means that God is involved in every part and place of your life. It means that we consult God more. For instance – God, is this the place you want me to go? Is this the thing you want me to do? God, can I agree to this contract? What is it that You would have me to do?

Keep your conversation open. Prayer is a conversation and we must learn to keep it open and flowing with God. Also, remember that it includes *active* listening and Holy Spirit said to me - we **need to hear God out on some things!** God has heard you. He has heard your prayer. He has heard your petition. He has heard your complaint. He has heard everything that you had to say, and we must

3

move into the prayer of listening and hear God out on some things.

We need to spend just as much time or more listening in prayer, as we do talking. Being open to God and full of prayer allows God to lead us in any given moment. It opens us up to more of His direction and His will. It takes us from a place of wondering to a place of knowing!

**Prayer Point:** Father, help me to remain in communication with You. Help me to spend time listening to what You have to say, in Jesus name!

Prayer is our door way to help!

*Romans 8:26-27 TLB - And in the same way - by our faith the Holy Spirit helps us with our daily problems and in our praying. For we don't even know what we should pray for nor how to pray as we should, but the Holy Spirit prays for us with such feeling that it cannot be expressed in words. And the Father who knows all hearts knows, of course, what the Spirit is saying as he pleads for us in harmony with God's own will.*

Some people are not praying because they feel they don't know how. Others feel they don't know what to pray. Some feel that prayer is a weak area for them. If this is you, will you allow God to help you?

Holy Spirit is our help in prayer! The text says Holy Spirit is our help with daily problems and in our praying! Don't allow not knowing what to say in prayer or feeling weak in the area of prayer to keep you from praying! The *New Living Translation* explains it like this - *And the Holy Spirit helps us in our weakness. For example, we don't know what God wants us to pray for. But the Holy Spirit prays for us with groanings that cannot be expressed in words.*

Here is a quick prayer! ***Prayer Point*** - Holy Spirit help me pray. Help me to pray all the time. When I don't know what to pray, help me. Holy Spirit pray for me! God, I don't know what You want me to pray but I know You want me to pray, so Holy Spirit help me, in Jesus name, Amen!

I told you that prayer is our door way to help! Philippians 4:6-7 shows us what prayer will add to our cup!

*Philippians 4:6-7 NLT - Don't worry about anything; instead, pray about everything. Tell God what you need and thank him for all he has done. Then you will experience God's peace, which exceeds anything we can understand. His peace will guard your hearts and minds as you live in Christ Jesus.*

This gives us more instructions on how to use this key, how this key helps us to keep our cup filled and what this key adds to our cup. There are benefits that come with using prayer to keep our cup filled. We already know - never stop praying and pray all the time. Now, the word instructs us to pray about everything!

But, why? There is purpose in unending, relentless prayer! This scripture says don't worry about anything, instead pray about everything. Tell God what you need and thank him for all He has done – *THEN* - meaning this is what happens as a result of prayer – this is the help that comes from prayer – peace is added to our cup!

*Then* you *will* experience peace that surpasses all understanding. Not only does prayer add peace to our cup, it also adds protection for our heart and mind! The scripture is clear. Then you will experience peace that will guard your hearts and minds as you live in Christ Jesus! We can use prayer to unlock the peace that we may have been missing in our life. We can use prayer to unlock protection from God. Prayer affects how we live in Christ. It affects our everyday lives and adds things that we sometimes can't see that we need, or don't know how to get.

When we keep our cups full, we lack nothing! This is why we can't give up in prayer!

*Colossians 4:2 TLB - Don't be weary in prayer; keep at it; watch for God's answers, and remember to be thankful when they come.*

Many people have become tired in prayer. Maybe you've gotten weary because you've been praying and haven't seen anything.

Yet, the instructions for our filled cup is to keep at it! We can't give up in prayer. We can't put down this key that is necessary to filling our cup. According to God's Word, we must continue to utilize the key of prayer and watch for God's answers because they will come! That's a promise that is attached to us remaining in prayer.

The text says to remember to be thankful *when* they come! We can't give up in prayer because prayer keeps us vigilant! Prayer keeps us sober! Prayer keeps us watching! If you're going to pray about it, keep at it, because the promise is – it, whatever your "it" is, will come!

If you are the person whose cup may be empty or half- filled because you've stopped believing that it was coming - be encouraged!! Maybe you put down your key of prayer because you haven't seen the answer yet. I speak into your life now - it's coming! Get back in prayer! Get back on the watch so that as you're watching, you're not lacking what you need while you wait!

This leads us to the final point of the prayer key.

*Mark 1:35 NLT - Before daybreak the next morning, Jesus got up and went out to an isolated place to pray.*

This is an important part of using this key: Make time to pray! Learn how to pull away from everything and everybody and give yourself to prayer. *Colossians 4:2(a) NIV says – Devote yourselves to prayer.* Not just any prayer, but time alone; away from people, away from the noise of the world and life and make time to pray! We put everything on our to do list but prayer! We carve out time for everything and everybody but God!

Before daybreak Jesus got up and went to pray! Some of us have good intentions but we're tied to the bed.

Has that been you? Have you forfeited times of prayer because you felt you were too tired or too sleepy to pray? Have you dismissed times of prayer because you didn't know what to pray?

Whatever our reasons may have been, if we're going to fill our cup, we must get up and go into the closet, the den, the prayer room or wherever we pray!

Get up and make time to pray!

# KEY TWO
## *Stay Connected To God*

The second Key is – Stay Connected To God! We started with prayer because prayer is the first way that we stay connected to God!

*John 15:1-16 NLT - "I am the true grapevine, and my Father is the gardener. He cuts off every branch of mine that doesn't produce fruit, and he prunes the branches that do bear fruit so they will produce even more. You have already been pruned and purified by the message I have given you. Remain in me, and I will remain in you. For a branch cannot produce fruit if it is severed from the vine, and you cannot be fruitful unless you remain in me.*

*"Yes, I am the vine; you are the branches. Those who remain in me, and I in them, will produce much fruit. For apart from me you can do nothing. Anyone who does not remain in me is thrown away like a useless branch and withers. Such branches are gathered into a pile to be burned. But if you remain in me and my words remain in you, you may ask for anything you want, and it will be granted! When you produce much fruit, you are my true disciples. This brings great glory to my Father.*

*"I have loved you even as the Father has loved me. Remain in my love. When you obey my commandments, you remain in my love, just as I obey my Father's commandments and remain in his love. I have told you these things so that you will be filled with my joy. Yes, your joy will overflow! This is my*

*commandment: Love each other in the same way I have loved you. There is no greater love than to lay down one's life for one's friends. You are my friends if you do what I command. I no longer call you slaves, because a master doesn't confide in his slaves. Now you are my friends, since I have told you everything the Father told me. You didn't choose me. I chose you. I appointed you to go and produce lasting fruit, so that the Father will give you whatever you ask for, using my name."*

*Connection Matters and Produces!*

According to the text in verse 2, when we use staying connected as a key to keep our cup filled, this key adds *pruning* and *producing* to our cup! **He cuts off every branch of mine that doesn't produce fruit, and he prunes the branches that do bear fruit so they will produce even more.**

Oftentimes pruning is seen as a bad thing. However, viewing this in the proper perspective, we learn that God cuts off what does not produce. He prunes what does so that it can produce more. Staying connected to God will ensure that whatever and whoever doesn't produce fruit will be cut off. It also ensures that our branches will produce more!

Jesus said, "**Yes, I am the vine; you are the branches. Those who remain in me, and I in them, will produce much fruit. For apart from me you can do nothing.**

Here is a quick **Prayer Point!** Father Help me to stay in You! I yield to Your pruning process. Cut off everything that is not producing good fruit for You. Add pruning to my cup so that I can produce more, in Jesus name, Amen.

Staying connected also adds *access* to our cup! See verse 7 - "**But if you remain in me and my words remain in you, you may ask for anything you want, and it will be granted!**"

There is a **YES** in your connection! You won't find the YES that you need on the outside of God! Not only will staying connected give you access to what you need, but you'll have access to what you want. Jesus said IF we remain in Him, and His words remain in us, we may ask for anything we **want** and it will be granted.

Staying connected adds *joy* to your cup! Look at verses 9-11. *"I have loved you even as the Father has loved me. Remain in my love. When you obey my commandments, you remain in my love, just as I obey my Father's commandments and remain in his love. I have told you these things so that you will be filled with my joy. Yes, your joy will overflow!*

Another quick **Prayer Point**! God, add joy to my cup!! In Jesus name, Amen!

Yes, it's just that simple! God will hear and honor our sincere, heartfelt prayer toward Him.

Do you see how prayer is so necessary in this walk?

Jesus also said we should remain in His love. When we stay connected, the joy of the Lord will flood our life. Those places meant to destroy our joy and send us into depression and despair will be flooded with joy. The key is to remain! To consistently be in the presence and the love of Jesus. Jesus said YES! Our joy will overflow! Joy – it's beyond happiness! Joy- it's not based on circumstance but it's in spite of it!

**Prayer Point!** Father, I will remain in You! Thank You for adding joy to my cup as I sit in Your presence and stay connected through Your love.

Staying connected also produces lasting fruit! It is important that we examine our fruit. Not only does God want us to produce good fruit, but lasting fruit. Fruit that will benefit and bless others beyond ourselves and long after we've gone on.

Staying connected creates relationship and a change of status. See verses 14-15 - ***You are my friends if you do what I command. I no longer call you slaves, because a master doesn't confide in his slaves. Now you are my friends, since I have told you everything the Father told me.***

If you ***do*** what I command! Staying connected includes remaining in obedience! It means doing what God calls us to do, when He tells us, and how He tells us!

Staying connected through obedience changes your status! Jesus said, "I no longer call you slaves – Now, you are my friends!" Obedience positions us for elevation from God! Too many people want elevation in their cup without having obedience in their cup! I encourage you to add obedience to your cup! This is something that we must be willing to do. Obey Gods' commands. Not just because it will benefit us, but because we love Him and want to please Him.

***Prayer Point!*** Father show me the ways that I have not obeyed! Forgive me and help me to realign myself in obedience with Your will and commands. I desire to be a friend to You, God. Help me in all of my ways to obey You. In Jesus name, Amen!

# KEY THREE
## *Obedience*

Key three is Obedience!

*Genesis 17:1 TLB - When Abram was ninety-nine years old, God appeared to him and told him, "I am the Almighty; obey me and live as you should.*

Obedience is a lifestyle!

God told Abram, "obey me and live as you should!" It's not an occasion or something that happens by chance. Obedience is a way of life. YOU must add it to your cup! How we live is important to God. What we do while we live is important to God. Living in obedience to God is a blessing to our lives even when we don't see it.

*Genesis 22:1-3 TLB - Later on, God tested Abraham's faith and obedience. "Abraham!" God called. "Yes, Lord?" he replied. "Take with you your only son - yes, Isaac whom you love so much - and go to the land of Moriah and sacrifice him there as a burnt offering upon one of the mountains which I'll point out to you!" The next morning Abraham got up early, chopped wood for a fire upon the altar, saddled his donkey, and took with him his son Isaac and two young men who were his servants, and started off to the place where God had told him to go.*

This is what obedience looks like. God says it and we do it! Sometimes obedience will require us to give up some things and some people. Sometimes obedience may be required without full understanding. Often, we are tempted to ask God why. While there is absolutely no harm in asking God questions, there is a difference when we question God. Many of us will delay our obedience or simply not obey because of a lack of understanding, but we must have faith to obey!

Obedience to God should also be immediate even when we don't fully understand God's why! God will make it make sense when it's time.

During one of my messages, God asked us – why are you praying about instructions from the God who gave you the instructions? Let that sink in!

Is it possible that you've turned prayer into an excuse to delay your obedience?

Again, obedience is - God said it and we get up and go!

***Prayer Point –*** Father, help me to readily obey You even when I don't understand Your why! Help me to obey You quickly and willingly. I desire to live as I should according to Your will, and have a lifestyle of obedience to You, in Jesus name. Amen.

***Exodus 6:10-12 TLB - Now the Lord spoke to Moses again and told him, "Go back again to Pharaoh and tell him that he must let the people of Israel go." "But look," Moses objected, "my own people won't even listen to me anymore; how can I expect Pharaoh to? I'm no orator!"***

This is another view of what obedience looks like. Even when it seems impossible - we still do it! Obedience requires us to confront the hard things, places and people. Obedience requires us to get beyond our own objections and excuses. And obedience will require us to get beyond ourselves and "the people!"

Moses said, "my own people won't even listen to me anymore;

how can I expect Pharaoh to? I'm no orator." Another version says, "I'm a clumsy speaker." Regardless of what people may do or say and regardless of how we see ourselves, we must fill our cups with obedience!

If we obey God, what we need, when we need it, will be available! We know this by the next verse in that account.

***Exodus 6:13 TLB – "Then the Lord ordered Moses and Aaron to return to the people of Israel and to Pharaoh, king of Egypt, demanding that the people be permitted to leave."***

God gave Moses some **HELP!** Many times the help that we need is found on the other side of our obedience to God.

Have you considered that your help may be delayed due to a lack of obedience? Is it possible that your help may be delayed because you've made excuses about why you couldn't obey God?

***Prayer Point*** - Lord, help me to fill my cup with obedience. I trust and believe that Your help will come! Help me to overcome what I believe are shortcomings about myself. Help me to overcome my fear of what others will think or say. I want to walk in full obedience to You. In Jesus name, Amen!

In addition to God's help, obedience also opens the door to healing and God's providential care!

***Exodus 15:26 TLB* - "If you will listen to the voice of the Lord your God, and obey it, and do what is right, then I will not make you suffer the diseases I sent on the Egyptians, for I am the Lord who heals you."***

Obedience requires listening and doing!

Our obedience must show up in our actions as well as our words. If we will fill our cup with obedience - listening and doing - God will add provision, protection, help and healing.

While we should obey God because we love Him and want to please Him, have you considered the benefits of willingly obeying God? Have you considered what you may be forfeiting simply because you've failed to obey God? Again, obedience is a blessing to our lives, though many times we don't recognize it.

The benefits of obedience are endless!

***Prayer Point*** - Father, as I obey You, I trust that Your will is right for me. Thank You for Your divine provision, protection, help and healing! Thank You, Lord, for helping me to see how obedience pleases You and benefits me. May my life be full of Your great benefits as I seek to fully obey You, in Jesus name! Amen.

# KEY FOUR
## *Eliminate the Distractions and*
## *Turn Off the Noise in Your Life*

The fourth key is Eliminating the Distractions and Turning Off the Noise in Your Life.

*Mark 4:18-19 NLT - The seed that fell among the thorns represents others who hear God's word, but all too quickly the message is crowded out by the worries of this life, the lure of wealth, and the desire for other things, so no fruit is produced.*

*Mark 4:18-19 TLB - The thorny ground represents the hearts of people who listen to the Good News and receive it, but all too quickly the attractions of this world and the delights of wealth, and the search for success and lure of nice things come in and crowd out God's message from their hearts, so that no crop is produced.*

The noise in our lives makes the ground in our lives unstable! The noise in our lives makes our ground thorny and unable to hold the seed of the Word when we receive it. Eliminating distractions and turning off the noise increases our capacity to receive from God!

YOU have to turn off the noise! YOU have to decide what's priority in your life! YOU have to decide what stays and what goes! You may need to put social media on MUTE! You may need to put some of the people in your life on MUTE so you can get YOUR ground right!

The text says - **all too quickly the message is crowded out by the worries of this life, the lure of wealth, and the desire for other things, so no fruit is produced.**

When we fail to add the elimination of distractions to our cup, we fail to produce fruit! But if we eliminate the distractions and turn down the noise this is what it will produce:

*Romans 12:2 NLT – Don't copy the behavior and customs of this world, but let God transform you into a new person by changing the way you think. Then you will learn to know God's will for you, which is good and pleasing and perfect.*

It will produce transformation! It will produce a NEW you! It will change the way you think! Then you will learn to know God's will for YOU! If you're seeking God's will for your life for real – turn the noise down! It will transform your life! The will of God for you will become known as God changes you and your mind!

But How?

*Hebrews 12:2 TLB - Keep your eyes on Jesus, our leader and instructor. He was willing to die a shameful death on the cross because of the joy he knew would be His afterwards; and now He sits in the place of honor by the throne of God.*

Eliminate the distractions by keeping your eyes on Jesus, our leader and instructor.

How? In prayer. Through obedience. And by staying connected!

*Mark 6:31 TLB - Then Jesus suggested, "Let's get away from the crowds for a while and rest." For so many people were coming and going that they scarcely had time to eat.*

The bottom line is that we need to pull away!

For many people, the crowd is our distraction! We need REST! Unfortunately, we've used excuses such as – "I can't be gone too long" or "I'll lose followers"- especially in this social media driven world we live in. Beloved, that means we **need** to be away, especially if we're worried about losing followers! We're supposed to be pointing them to Jesus! We must remember that we are **A** Voice, not **THE** Voice!

Pull away and eliminate the distraction of the crowd. The crowd just may have too much priority in your life! Is it possible that you could be listening more to the crowd, than you are to God?

***Prayer Point!*** Lord, help me to pull away and turn off the noise in my life. Anything that is noisy and preventing me from receiving from You, uncover it so that I can pull away. Forgive me for making the crowd a greater priority than You, in Jesus name. Amen!

***Matthew 6:31-33 TLB - "So don't worry at all about having enough food and clothing. Why be like the heathen? For they take pride in all these things and are deeply concerned about them. But your heavenly Father already knows perfectly well that you need them, and He will give them to you if you give Him first place in your life and live as He wants you to.***

Simply said - eliminating the distractions and turning off the noise in our life helps us to put Him in first place, and live as He wants us to.

So many people can't live right because they have the wrong little gods in first place! The little god of social media. The little god of what everybody else is doing. The little god of busyness of doing the work. The little god of people pleasing. These little gods have us worrying about things that our BIG God already has under control! Things like - how are they going to see me? What are they going to think about how I look, or what I'm wearing? What if my hair isn't right? Are my nails done or do I have a fresh cut?

The little gods may be making too much noise in your life. It's time to eliminate them!

***Prayer Point:*** Father, I repent!! Forgive me for every little god that I've given first place and more priority than You! I willingly renounce every little god. I cast down everything that wants to exalt itself against the knowledge of God. I declare, right now, that You are the only Lord of my life! I declare, right now, that every little god that has been given rank in my life is dethroned now, in Jesus name! I yield to You and Your word. I submit myself to Your will for me. Every noise that is not the sound of heaven must be silenced, in Jesus name! Thank You for correcting and redirecting me back to You, in Jesus name! Amen!

# KEY FIVE
## *Mind Your Own Business*

When God gave me this message and said this is a key to keeping my cup filled, I said - OH! Oh really God! And God said YES! Mind Your Own Business! This is key five!

**Proverbs 26:17 NLT - *Interfering in someone else's argument is as foolish as yanking a dog's ears.***

So many people have their hands and their mouths in things they have absolutely no business in! It has nothing to do with them. They aren't experts on the matter. They simply "have something to say." The truth is, just because we have something we'd like to say, doesn't mean that we should.

Some are getting bitten because they are interfering in someone else's argument or someone else's business. As it relates to the body of Christ, everything is not for us to respond to, comment on and definitely not to preach about!

**John 21:22 NLT - *Jesus replied, "If I want him to remain alive until I return, what is that to you? As for you, follow Me."***

Jesus was talking to Peter who was questioning him about what someone else was doing. His response was - what is **that** to **you?**

*Please note – I have written this statement just as I heard the Lord say it!* The Lord said – Get you some MIND YOUR BUSINESS and fill your cup with THAT!

Everything is not for us to speak on, to address or to deal with!

Jesus told Peter – As for YOU - follow Me!

Too many people are engaged in catfights, arguments, disputes and debates and the Lord said – WHAT IS THAT TO YOU? The devil is literally laughing at the body of Christ as we jump on bandwagons, entertaining foolish arguments about things that are not beneficial or helpful to the body of Christ. It does more harm than good, and unfortunately, we don't use or have enough wisdom or discernment to realize it.

It's time to stop being a busy body and a know-it-all and worry about yourself! Worry about *your* obedience! Worry about *your* prayer life! Worry about *your* connection!

If God has not assigned you to it, what is it to you? If it has nothing to do with what God has commissioned you to do – mind your business. Don't allow yourself to continue to be distracted by people and things that are not a part of your mandate or mission in the earth.

*1 Thessalonians 4:11-12 NLT - Make it your goal to live a quiet life, minding your own business and working with your hands, just as we instructed you before. Then people who are not believers will respect the way you live, and you will not need to depend on others.*

When we add Minding Your Business to your cup, it means working with our hands as we've been instructed.

What has God instructed you to do that you haven't done? Maybe you've been too preoccupied with everybody else's business? Have you exerted all of your energy in other places but not enough on the things God has assigned to you?

I know this verse isn't popular because it tells us to live a quiet life when the world continuously says make some noise. We have to know when to make noise and about what. Not everything requires us to make noise and not every time. Take a moment to consider the things you may **not** be doing while you're meddling in things that have nothing to do with you.

Beloved, it's okay to stay in your lane and do what God has given your hands to do. That's where you'll be more effective and have greater influence and impact.

**My specific prayer: Lord, may this part of the revelation help someone as they read it.**

There are people who can't understand why others can't "get with them" or won't connect with them. It could possibly be that they have no respect for how you live! Whoa! It's right there in verse 12.

**"Then people who are _not believers_ will respect the way you live."**

Have you ever considered that minding your own business or not doing so is an indication of how you live **and** that it could help or hinder others? Is it possible that you're not able to effectively reach unbelievers because they see how you live and have no desire to meet your God? Is it possible that you are guilty of causing people to not desire salvation **or** God because they see how you live?

We must represent Jesus in what we say and what we do! We have a responsibility to draw others to Christ through our living! Your very life, how you live - could be the very witness that someone needs to see or encounter to help them make the life altering decision to accept Jesus as their Lord.

**Prayer Point** – In the name of the Lord Jesus Christ, help me to mind my own business. Lord, reveal to me where I may have been a hindrance to anyone encountering or accepting You as their Lord. Forgive me if I've meddled in things that were not my business. Forgive me if how I have lived has caused non-believers to reject

You. Help me to correct it today, in Jesus name! Help me to live in a way that is pleasing to You and exalts You as the Lord of my life.

Now - the good news is - there is a way to rectify the problem.

*2 Thessalonians 3:11-12 TLB - Yet we hear that some of you are living in laziness, refusing to work, and wasting your time in gossiping. In the name of the Lord Jesus Christ we appeal to such people - we command them - to quiet down, get to work, and earn their own living.*

Close your mouth! Stop being lazy! Get to work!

If you're reading this book and you know that you're a gossiper – Stop!

Repent!

Quiet down and do YOUR Work!

If you've been lazy – Repent! It's a waste of time! Time is a currency of the Kingdom that should not be wasted but used wisely. Always remember that once we've spent your time, we can never recoup it.

Consider this: Are you wasting time on things that are not adding value to others' lives and the Kingdom of God?

Even as a part of the Kingdom of God, it doesn't give us a right to jump into every fight or voice our thoughts on every matter. I know some believe that the Kingdom is *your* business! However, I beg to differ. The Kingdom of God belongs to God!

We are employed by God to do our work in the Kingdom as designated by Him. That includes minding our business and not being busy bodies. Being a busy body is a distraction that many need to eliminate!

**Prayer Point** – Lord, help me to get to work! If I've wasted the precious time you've given me by gossiping, being lazy or any other way that's displeasing to You, I repent. Forgive me and help me to correct my behavior. Change my heart, my words and my actions in Jesus name! Help me to eliminate the distraction of being in others business and not minding my own. Forgive me for the times I felt the need to speak on things whether they concerned me or not. Help me to understand that a reaction from me is not always necessary. Pull me out of anything that has nothing to do with me and is not giving You the glory, in Jesus name!

# KEY SIX
## *Fasting*

Key six helps us with all of the previous keys!

FASTING!

*1 Corinthians 9:27 NLT - I discipline my body like an athlete, training it to do what it should. Otherwise, I fear that after preaching to others I myself might be disqualified.*

Most people need to add discipline to their cup. We literally need to train ourselves to pray. Train ourselves to stay connected. Train ourselves to obey. Train ourselves to eliminate distractions. We can do this through developing a lifestyle of fasting.

To train means to make proficient by instruction and practice! Instruction *and* practice! Hearing *and* doing! Too often, God's people have no discipline in the things and ways of God. We have not developed in critical areas of our walk with God because we have not done the work.

Not only should fasting be a discipline in our lives, fasting helps to develop discipline in other areas of our lives!

*James 4:8-10 TLB - And when you draw close to God, God will draw close to you. Wash your hands, you sinners, and let your hearts be filled with God alone to make them pure and true to him. Let there be tears for the wrong things you have done. Let there be sorrow and sincere grief. Let there be sadness instead of laughter, and gloom instead of joy. Then when you realize your worthlessness before the Lord, he will lift you up, encourage and help you.*

*James 4:8-10 NLT - Come close to God, and God will come close to you. Wash your hands, you sinners; purify your hearts, for your loyalty is divided between God and the world. Let there be tears for what you have done. Let there be sorrow and deep grief. Let there be sadness instead of laughter, and gloom instead of joy. Humble yourselves before the Lord, and he will lift you up in honor.*

Fasting is necessary so that we can empty ourselves out and be filled and refilled. Be fueled and refueled! Fasting is necessary so that we can draw close to God and God can draw close to us! God doesn't only draw close to us when we're broken hearted. Fasting opens the door for intimacy with God, but *we* have to open the door!

Fasting also produces purity. Purity is freedom from anything that debases, contaminates, pollutes, etc... Fasting helps to purify our thoughts and brings clarity. When we fast, it changes what and how we think and speak.

Do you know the areas in your life that may need purification through fasting before the Lord?

Adding fasting to our cup also produces FREEDOM! Freedom from what has debased us – meaning to reduce in quality or value. Freedom from what has reduced us in quality or value. Fasting restores our value!

Can you think of places in your life that have been devalued? Maybe places that you have devalued simply because life happened. Fasting can help you in this area.

Fasting also produces freedom from what has contaminated us. Contaminated means to make impure or unsuitable by contact or mixture with something unclean, bad, etc. Contaminated also means to render harmful or unusable.

Fasting frees us from things, ties, places, people, and/or actions that have made us impure and unsuitable, harmful and unusable!

Fasting makes YOU a better YOU!

Also – fasting produces freedom from what pollutes us! Pollute means to make morally unclean; to defile.

TRUE FASTING WILL CLEAN YOU UP!

It empties us of things that debase, contaminate and pollute us, creating space for GOD! It creates space for the heart of God, the mind of God and help *from* God!

Fasting cleans out the harmful, unstable things within us so we can be filled with God and what's good! Fasting helps us draw close to the Father! It removes barriers and hindrances *within* us.

*Acts 13:2-3 TLB - One day as these men were worshiping and fasting the Holy Spirit said, "Dedicate Barnabas and Paul for a special job I have for them." So after more fasting and prayer, the men laid their hands on them - and sent them on their way.*

This is one of the results of fasting. These verses demonstrate how God will help us and direct our decisions. Fasting unlocks answers. Fasting helps us make the GOD decision. It helps us to make the decision that is in His will; the decision that will bring Him glory!

Have you submitted the decisions you're making to fasting? Is there some area that you really need help in, and you've done everything you could think of?

I encourage you to fill your cup with fasting.

## KEY SEVEN
### *Worship*

The seventh and final key is Worship!

Unfortunately, many don't worship because their perspective of worship is wrong. This scripture may help you.

*Numbers 28:1-2 NLT - The Lord said to Moses, "Give these instructions to the people of Israel: The offerings you present as special gifts are a pleasing aroma to me; they are my food. See to it that they are brought at the appointed times and offered according to my instructions."*

Worship is a pleasing aroma to God! Worship is God's food!

*Numbers 28:1-2 TLB* states it like this - *The Lord gave Moses these instructions to give to the people of Israel: "The offerings which you burn on the altar for me are my food, and are a pleasure to me; so see to it that they are brought regularly and are offered as I have instructed you.*

Worship should be done regularly. Our worship brings pleasure to God. And worship should be given to God as God instructs!

Here is a necessary truth concerning worship - how you worship may not look the way I worship! This is why it's so important to never criticize the worship of someone else because we don't know how God is leading them in worship! Worship is not what we've made it look like in today's worldview.

Worship is Holy Spirit led and should be intentional.

Worship also includes confession.

*Nehemiah 9:3 TLB - The laws of God were read aloud to them for two or three hours, and for several more hours they took turns confessing their own sins and those of their ancestors. And everyone worshiped the Lord their God.*

Too often we want the benefits of worship without the responsibility. We desire the times of refreshing from the presence of the Lord negating the need for confession.

Have you considered that making your confession before God is a way to worship Him; reverencing Him and your need of Him?

Worship includes acknowledging whatever wrong we may have done and sincerely releasing it to Him.

*Acts 3:19-20 NLT - Now repent of your sins and turn to God, so that your sins may be wiped away. Then times of refreshment will come from the presence of the Lord, and he will again send you Jesus, your appointed Messiah.*

Worship includes repentance. It includes turning away from sin and turning *to* God. Worship is not just our words but more important - our actions.

*Acts 3:19-20 TLB* states it like this - *Now change your mind and attitude to God and turn to him so he can cleanse away your sins and send you wonderful times of refreshment from the presence of the Lord and send Jesus your Messiah back to you again.*

Worship involves changing our mind and attitude *to* God. Worship produces cleansing and refreshment. We want refreshment but cleansing comes first.

Do you need to change your mind and attitude? This is an invitation to turn to Him. Allow Him to cleanse and refresh you in His presence.

There is one more scripture I'd like to share with you for this key.

*John 4:21-24 TLB - Jesus replied, "The time is coming, ma'am, when we will no longer be concerned about whether to worship the Father here or in Jerusalem. For it's not where we worship that counts, but how we worship - is our worship spiritual and real? Do we have the Holy Spirit's help? For God is Spirit, and we must have His help to worship as we should. The Father wants this kind of worship from us. But you Samaritans know so little about Him, worshiping blindly, while we Jews know all about Him, for salvation comes to the world through the Jews."*

As stated earlier, all of these keys give us access to our **help**! We must have His help (the Holy Spirit) to worship as we should! God is calling His people out of the formality of worship, the "presentation" that we've given Him and calling us back into Him. He's calling us to a place that worship will not just be something, we 'GO TO' or something we see as "what we do" but Worship will become a lifestyle! It will be our very nature. He's calling us to a place where worship with our Father is automatic, without needing prompting. He's calling us to a place where worship is what we literally feed to God daily as His food and for His pleasure.

## *Final Thoughts*

## *7 Keys to Keep Your Cup Filled!*

When we fill our cups with the help of Holy Spirit, everything is where we need it, when we need it! When we fill our cups, it will eliminate worry and stress. We'll be full of faith that God our provider has added to our cup based on what we've lifted up in our cup before Him!

### *7 Keys*

Prayer

Staying Connected To God

Obedience

Eliminating Distractions and Turn Off the Noise

Mind Your Own Business

Fasting

Worship

God's formula works if we will put in the work!

***James 2:17 NKJV- Thus also faith by itself, if it does not have works, is dead.***

I encourage you to activate these keys and fill your cup according to what God has prescribed. I decree that daily you will access what God Has laid up for you.

My prayer is that you will continuously be filled and remain full in Jesus name!

*LaTrice Williams*

# ABOUT THE AUTHOR

LaTrice Williams, The Destiny Driver, is God's servant first and foremost. She is Mom to many beautiful children, two of which she had biologically. She is Gigi to one beautiful granddaughter, one handsome grandson and Spiritual Mom to others.

LaTrice is gifted to the body of Christ as an Apostle and Prophet. She is the Apostolic Visionary and Sr. Pastor of *Divine Grace Ministries International* – Georgia, Louisiana and North Carolina. She is also the CEO and Founder of *LaTrice Williams Ministries* and *Living With More Enterprises*. She is the Founder of Destiny World Training Institute, equipping, training and building up strong, effective Kingdom Leaders. She is also the creator of #DestinyMoments, times that she uses to impart wisdom and help others navigate their destiny journey.

As one of God's chosen vessels, LaTrice loves sharing the Word of God through many avenues. She will literally preach and teach her shoes off as she endeavors to empower, encourage and strengthen others to pursue their destiny, live in wholeness, and receive the healing that is available for their lives.

### *Other Available Books by LaTrice Williams*

Hurt to Healing
Articles of Encouragement – 30 Days of Empowering You
Meditations - Heart, Mind and Soul
My Destiny Journal (full -sized journal)
Such A Long Night